I Don't Like It, You Can Do Better

Safaa A. Mahwi

GoToPublish LLC
1-888-337-1724
www.gotopublish.com
info@gotopublish.com

Contents

Introduction

What would you do if I gave you a chance to achieve something great? You might ask what could that be ???

To create human society all over again, according to your desires, and you would be the leader and teacher for that new community, you will create its rules and build its foundation. What will you do then?????? What will you add? What will you delete?

Note: I will state my opinion with all honesty without any fear or flattery because I am criticizing something wrong with very bad consequences.

Dedicate

To the human race

Thankfulness Appreciation

To the translator
Ryadh Al-Mandiwi

The Proofreader
Juliana Garcia

Cover designer
Safaa A.Mhawi

((1))

I don't know the cause but all I care about the result.

A very classy civilization was destroyed in the blink of an eye, the civilized people are now looking for some-thing to eat and drink, like the best wild animals. Only a few survived after the disaster. Because this creature is called "human" then he/she must be humane, enjoy the company of other humans, thus they started to look for one another, and every time they found someone they would feel very happy. My dad would laughing out loud saying: "We found one and lost billions...".

Some survivors witnessed the ancient era being destroyed by humans. They witnessed the huge scientific and technological advancement that the human made machines had reached; one of these people was my father.

My father was a very famous sociology professor and philosopher of his time. He wrote many thesis and oversaw many studies at many universities: "Hahaha, there was a time that we used to play, and now the times are toying with us" he always repeated that sentence.

Our numbers started to increase. We chose a nice place to live. the place was a green piece of land next to a river, stable weather, it contained some caves that were suitable for living. Sometimes we made trips to the nearby old cities that had high rise buildings (the ones that survived the disaster). We enjoyed these trips some time we found weird metal, ceramic, and plastic objects. We threw some of them without knowing if they were valuable or not. We kept others that we found to be interesting or something we could recognize. We had a lot of fun doing that.

The thing that made me and my father feel the happiest, was the big library we found underneath one of the buildings. The library survived the looting simply because it was the last thing anyone would think of stealing at that time, thus it was left intact. I'm an excellent reader, I had some education as a student in one of the well-known schools, before the disaster. When we found that library, I was so excited to continue my education especially at a difficult time like this. The library contained thousands of books, but I brought only one book back, when my father saw that book he smiled and said "You brought the best book of the library…. The library's index is a great idea so we can choose the best books in your new library."

We sat together for many nights picking the books we liked. We created a long list of books and decided to bring them back all at once, as well as some shelves to keep the books. We made one trip to bring the books, and then we started reading them, so the journey of reading and learning began.

We also brought our basic and important needs from the nearby cities such as medicine, handy tools, flashlights, nonperishable food, and other necessities.

"This is good. Our community is starting to grow wonderfully. The best part is that they are organized and not chaotic, despite the circumstances that we suffered my son." "Yes father, the best part is that we secured our basic needs. The agriculture experience was more than wonderful."

"When humans fill their stomachs, they start feeding their brains, When they use their brains, they start searching for luxury and sophistication in present life and in preparation for future plans. Future plans... this is what I would like to start discussing with you thoroughly and in depth.

"I am ready Father"

"Alright... you have a lot of good characteristics; wisdom, common sense, and logical thinking that allowed you to gain everyone's' trust. They consider you their leader and their role model, they ask for your advice and opinion about every small and big matter. All of that gives you a great opportunity to be a leader and teacher for our new society for which you establish the correct moral code and remove the bad behaviors. I don't deny that it will be a huge responsibility, moreover, extremely precise and sensitive.

"What you plant today you will harvest tomorrow."

"How do I start Father??"

"In order to create a successful prosperous future, you must benefit from the experiences of the past, adopt the good, and of course, dismiss the bad." "Hahaha, of course I won't find any-one better than you to talk about the experiences of the past, to analyze in detail."

"First of all Son, you must realize that humans are creatures who love good noble moral values. This is how humans feel when they are satisfied, and when they door to their desires is still locked. But once the door for desires and whims is open, haha, then they start Compromising their morals and principles, or they will falls from them principles when they are running after these desires and whims in the long long track of life, thus when you accumulate enough information and a clear vision of the human nature, you will know the results of what you will provide for the society, and its reflection on the people.

Be very very careful with everything you say, be aware of the ideas and opinions you propose."

"What I am about to say is not necessarily applicable to a big community, but you can start it in your own home, planting righteous morals and preparing a pure environment so your children will grow the right way and become valuable to themselves and others."

"Alright Father, how will you start with me?"

"We will start discussing the basis and corner stones of a society first."

"Good, let's put together a plan now, we will start discussing the details to-morrow after dinner, After we finish our daily routines, we will meet in my house for the discussion."

"Excellent, the invitation is open to everyone, for maximum benefit. Goodnight."

((3))

After we finished our daily errands, we headed to my father's place. He was waiting for us. Young girls pre-pared the place in a nice and com-fort-able way. The place was vibrant clean, there were dim lights, comfortable soft seats, big fancy chair for my father in the middle of the room, food and drinks were prepared, everyone was grateful and happily participated in this event. My father took the podium and started talking clearly and steadily.

My father was not only a very articulate speaker, but rather the best speaker ever. He knows exactly how to captivate an audience and connect relevant content while focusing on the main message of his speech. He knows how to keep an audience wholeheartedly intrigued and enthralled, At the same time he avoids the monotonous, boring, and irrelevant details.

"Dear compatriots, we survived a lot of obstacles after the disaster, We managed to keep a source of supplies and necessities, thus we accomplished a great success, As I have just said, we survived a lot of obstacles but these obstacles never end. Human ambition, which is what pushes us to do our best, is also a source of these obstacles, this is one side, the other side is ... sticking by the morals and sublime principles in a society that does not appreciate these morals and principles, is a source of hardships.

Here lies our dual responsibility first is to establish the high principles and ethics, Secondly, substantiate the way to establish these morals and principles in order for them to prosper and be useful in society.

The beautiful part is that we are not far from an integrated society, a new experiment rich with both its positive and negative aspects. Most of us have lived through and witnessed these days.

The good person is the one who learns lessons from others' mistakes without repeating that mistake personally. The first thing that humans started regulating was the ((law)) which is a set of general rules and regulations that is placed to organize people's rights and to punish the violators of those rules.

Those rules would be established ac-cording to the best interest of the general public, or what serves the purpose of some. Thus I will not go into deeper details about the topic of the law, be-cause it is subject to a lot of countless variables.

The big societies usually have a legislative authority that regulates rules and courts to question and punish the violators. And finally the executive authority that is in charge of enforcing these rules and penalties that were issues by the courts. Now, let's start with the important basics of the human society.

((4))

Education

Society is filled with a variety of jobs and careers. However, three of these jobs are considered the most noble in human society. Those jobs are the doctor, the judge, and the teacher. Thus, teaching is one of the most important corner stones of society, moreover, it is the main corner stone. You must handle it with utmost care; teaching a child from young age is like engraving on stone. I have always seen this proverb to be very expressive of the importance of teaching and its role in our lives.

As I have mentioned previously, we must be aware of what ideas and values we establish. Here lays the responsibility of raising and educating our offspring.

Education interacts with the minds of children, which are fresh, open, playful, fertile minds, ready for any ideas to be planted regardless of the type of idea. The most dangerous part is that these young minds are very willing to accept any ideas spontaneously and defend these ideas regardless of how controversial these ideas are.

Here is some advice to anyone who wants to rule the world:

"Dear tyrant, if you want to rule the world and impose your authority, all you have to do is raise a generation and teach them your morals and ideas, then stay patient for twenty years until they become an invincible unbeatable army. Even if you lose a battle, you will never lose the war."

This is the importance and the risk of education.

One of the other things I wanted to mention to you, is the suffering of the refugees and the immigrants who were displaced from their own countries by force. Had to flee to new countries away from home.

They are aliens in their language, thinking, religion, culture and..... education. They were able to learn the language and adapt to a new ways of life. They kept their culture and religion, yet the only obstacle that they cannot overcome is the education. So you can imagine how these parents feel when they see their precious offspring graduating from school after gaining the best degrees addition to morals and values that are very different from the morals which they were raised and have lived. These parents had hoped that their children would continue their cultural inheritance.

Should they be happy that their children gained this education? or be sad because the minds of children are now filled with new and strange ideas on them.

This always leads to the parents either keeping silent because of the fear of problems, or Getting into trouble that ends in various ways and with great losses.

Thus I wrote a long letter to the education staff at that time, the summary of that letter was as follows: "Dear esteemed teachers,

I look like you as a good gardener in simple clothes and pure calming smile. A shepherd wakes up before sunrise and goes to his filed which is full of beautiful flowers and ripe plants. He spends hours and days and months and years, forgetting his own issues and burdens, in order to take care of his plants and flowers. He spends his precious life to tend to his field.

The flowers of your field are the best parts of ourselves, they are our offspring. How many teachers have become like parents to tens and hundreds of the children they taught. The most beautiful part about teaching children is when you see them acquiring skills, experiences, adopting your teachings and when they consider these parental teachings as a sacred constitution. Thus, ladies and gentlemen, I hope you pay attention to what information you plant in our children's heads.

The plants stay in the farm but your students come back home at the end of the day.

I hope you become aware of the impact of what you plant, and I am sure that you are very cautious already, as none of you want these ideas to grow into invasive weed in the student's head which might cause misery to his or her family.

These children are entrusted to you and I am very confident that you are up to the responsibility of that trust.

Accept my deepest regards gratitude."

My father stayed quiet for few moments. Then he said "This is enough for today, I will see you all tomorrow"

((5))

Nurturing and rehabilita-
tion of women

When we speak about women, we are not only talking about half the human society, as I consider women to be the foundation of society.

She is the being that embodies multiple beautiful contradictions at the same time!!! You see her being romantic sensitive soft dreamer, while at tough times she is the opposite. She switches from softness and sweetness to the utmost power and toughness.

From dreamer to realist and practical. From soft to tough and strict. From sensitive romantic to rough and fierce. She is the nucleus of the noblest component of the human society, the family.

When you raise those little girls who are playing now in front of you, you are actually preparing for the rise of the best and most successful families. Each one of them will become the tree, refuge, source of love, compassion, and affection. She will grow bright innocent eyes and start calling you the most beautiful words ever "Mom" and "Dad". Then they will grow and the older they get, the more responsibilities they will have. The most difficult period to raise a child is the age when they start making decisions. Who will they go to???

Thus, prepare your sons to be successful fathers and your daughters to be successful mothers. The first stage of preparation is school, which must include programs, instructions, guidance, and advice, but before that is preparing them at home.

I must mention something here; there used to be rehabilitation centers for girls who were involved in criminal activities. These centers used to rehabilitate these girls to live a new life and have a new start. However, these centers were not often successful because of the changes that happen to a person who is arrested, goes to trial, and then prison. Thus, a better idea would be to open new programs and create more job opportunities, as well as offer more guidance to the girls who need them, we would save many more girls from falling into the dark corners.

((6))

Religion

Historians had claimed that the primitive humans feared natural phenomena like fires, earthquakes, and volcanoes, thus these first humans started thinking that there are great invisible powers that controlled these phenomena. Then humans in-vented Gods and tried to get closer to them, thus a few primitive religions appeared, these religions are referred to as paganism by the later celestial religions.

Prophets... who said that they were messengers of a great God, powerful and with unparalleled qualities on earth. The creator of all creatures and the one who decided their fortune, future, prosperity, and purposes in life.

He is merciful and kind. He has the keys to heaven and luxuries unlike anything anyone has seen or can even imagine. He promised these heavens to good people who have done good and noble deeds.

He is an avenging Titan, who uses scorching fires that melt rocks and iron, the regular fire we see every day is nothing compared to that, as hell fire is thousands of times more intense, and he prepared that for infidels and criminals.

This is what they used to say with great confidence and faith. Truth be told, the religions do have good noble morals and values. Also the religions also have a complete set of rules and laws. Thus these religions were the best organizational side of society.

Many people were sincere in their worship, and reached the goal of dedication, devotion, and literal commitment, by applying the laws and laws of religion.

The amount of commitment to religion is related to the morals of the person himself. The more a person's morals and high respect for himself the more he is a good and kind person. He takes into account the rights of others and fears the God who worships him.

He may not be a hermit, a monk, a worshiper, but he has a good con-science and a kind heart.

The believers left in their worship many examples of great splendor and beauty, examples full of lessons and sermons that represent the highest values and lofty principles, and the beauty in this matter is that they did not want fame, or that their actions were immortal, and they were remembered over time ..... Noble, and kindness to them.

Some of them did not sleep at night, you see him sitting and praying. Some of them spent all their money to help the poor and feed the hungry. In them you will find someone who is sincere in advice and education and urges people to do good and stop hurting others. Among them are those who sacrificed themselves and their blood and severed their ties and killed those closest to him in front of his eyes......

All this is so that he does not say a single word that contradicts his con-science and his high noble morals, so those believers have become immortal suns that shine and are not absent in human history.

But as I told you that the matter is related to the person himself, as good people appeared, there were the opposite of those who took advantage of religion to become one of the fastest ways to get rich and achieve ultimate power and enjoy many other obscene pleasures. It has been Desecrated in the worst and lowest ways. Every religion (whether of earthly or divine origin) grew an inside layer of followers that benefited from it for their person-al legitimate and illegitimate gains.

They built big temples in cities so that many people visit those cities. That turned them into big commercial centers that contained all types of merchandise which were sold around the clock, and that brought back astronomical profits. Don't forget that temples need vast lands for agriculture and expansion. They also needed servants, guards, staff, administration, and accountants ...etc. That made it an independent and complete establishment that rivals the government of some countries. In some cases it surpassed the government. So in some countries you can find two authorities, one is civilian and the other is religious. Each one is trying to control the other. By the end, the results are a lot of victims.

The first victims ... The prophets themselves; Some of them were tortured in the most horrific ways. Drive by nails onto the wood. One of them was thrown alive into the burning bonfire. Another threw it into the raging sea, to be swallowed by a great whale. Another one he gets into a confrontation with his cousins. They got him a severe enmity he was forced him to leave his homeland for ten years.

How many were tortured to death, and killed with sword and poison.

When the situation settled down for the followers of one religion, they start fighting followers of other religions. In any way possible. First, they start with the propaganda to attempt to draw more followers to their religion. The funny ironic thing is, they use the same excuse, every time. And they keep using that same excuse for thousands of years. "We are the only legitimate religion that is accepted by God, and everyone else will go to hell, even if they believed in God but were one true religion." Does this sound right? I don't know.

I try to imagine myself in this situation, standing in front of God at doomsday and saying to Him" I believe in You and Your rules, and I surrendered myself to You, but I was born into (such and such) religion and did not follow this other religion, taking into consideration that all religions have the same source." I would expect Him to tell me: "You fool, haven't your people said in one of your proverbs 'all roads lead to Rome!?!? Then why do you ask???"

The next stage after the propaganda is questioning and doubting, and then slandering what the prophets says: "Your holy book is distorted, tampered, as it has been written by a human"

Then that leads to the philosophical analysis of every word that was mention in that holy book and religion. Then we compare this religion and that religion, and the benefits and gains you will get if you switched from your religion to MY religion.

Hahaha, that reminds me of the insurance and phone company advertisements, you will get hammered by many offers and promises of benefits and advantages, in most cases you can get the (golden offer) "Dear consumer, if you follow us you will get the ultimate salvation regardless of how many sins you had, you will not even be questioned about those sins!" What?????????

Does that mean that humans will stand before God while their hands are covered with blood knowing they had been the cause of misery to others, yet they are forgiven because they follow this or that group?

Wow, what a total divine justice!!! If this is the real divine justice then it can go to hell…

This is just a promotion and an aggravation to rebellion, sins, and criminal activities. The proof is that you can find some individuals who will reach to the level of killing themselves and everyone around them while totally convinced that this act is right and that what God had ordered and this will make them go to heaven.

5 stars brainwash.

Then this reaches the maximum, mass genocide and annihilation. Oh how much it hurts to remember indescribable crimes that were committed in the name of religion, in the name of a God that never ordered that. They claim that they are the soldiers of God in His land and that they were sent to spread His religion and divine heavenly instructions. Then they start by slaughtering those who oppose them as lambs are slaughtered, women were taken as captives and sold just as any other commodity, and they did the same to children.

"Had this really happened father? In the beginning, few thousand years ago?"

"Yes, and current historians called these (the dark ages) where humans were primitive, barbaric, and uncivilized, hahaha, then in the modern age some people started repeating these same barbaric and uncivilized behaviors!!!"

"Then why did you call these ages "dark" when you behaved just like them?? Moreover, some of you improvised terrifying methods that never even crossed the mind of Satan himself??"

WHY none of you are eager to go to these wonderfully described heavens?!!!

Why did you not imitate the believers and the pious who were among you?

WHY are none of you afraid of that hellish fire that melts steel and rocks???!!

Whom do you think you are deceiving?? You are only deceiving yourselves. We had enough of these lies. Every group is claiming that salvation is in their hands, if we follow that group and abided by their path.

Why should I wear your yoke of slavery around my neck? Who are you???? You claim that you are authorized by God and that we have to obey. Since when do you decide the condition of who is going to heaven or hell? You say that God had given you this right??? I swear to your God that you lied. We are all equal humans, we have equal rights and responsibilities, no one is higher than the other, no one owes anyone else for this. Everything you are saying is simply a propaganda to push for your allegations and excuses so that you can get to the head of power on the expense of other people's lives; you want to use the broken necks of others as a staircase to climb to the top.

This is what I used to tell them as loud as I could, but in vain, and then the worst happened...the followers of religions were divided into groups and sects, and this created more top positions to occupy by those who sought richness and power at the expense of the innocent people's lives. You cannot imagine the huge number of victims, millions of people died, there were rivers of blood, some of these groups started to get very creative in inventing new torture and terrorizing methods, even infants, the most innocent and beautiful creatures, were not safe from murder.

How much we ashamed when we stand facing your justice my lord?

Religion was a divine message that God had sent to his prophets to guide and educate humans; to put them on the path of virtue, peace, and prosperity. He did not send the religions to become a cause of death and destruction, or to be used as a method to gain power and persecute people, or make huge profits for small portion of the population on the expense of the majority.

I hope you take your time to imagine what had happened. I will see you tomorrow to finish talking about this, I will tell you about one reaction as a result of what had happened.

((7))

Atheism

I don't know how it began, or who created it the first time!? Was it a result
of the accumulation of religions and
the behaviors and power of the clergy-
men? Or is it a new independent idea?
Or is it the desire to live recklessly and
avoid responsibilities of our actions
and deeds? Or so not to worry about
the idea that there are angels who are
writing precise reports about everything you do, every word every glance,
even every evil thought in your head?
All of these reports are gathered in one
big book then it is held against you up
there, and your destiny It be-comes
dark colorless.

I do not deny that removing the responsibility and sins of humans shoul-
ders can give a comfort and relaxation. The problem is, no one had re-
turned from the dead to inform us if

this sense of relaxation is true, or is it the quiet the precedes the storm… no one knows.

Yesterday I told you about the heavy influence that religion has on society, and how it had been abused by those who benefited from it.

As a reaction, a group of people decided not to listen to any religious authority, and they went further to say that there is no such a thing as the creator of this world, it is just a lie that was created to become an excuse for some people so they can control us, and achieve person gains. Then it went even further to become an independent way of thinking that adapted a lot of philosophical controversial theories.

((There is no creator; we were created by nature. All creatures live their lives then died, that is it, and there is no life after death, no judgment after death))

If nature created us, then why it did not create other advanced and intelligent creatures?

Can't you see that this is not an odd coincidence?? Can't you understand that such intelligence and awareness is above average?

Many were attracted to the idea that nature created us, what support-ed that idea even more are the precise scientific theories that were discovered to explain the chemical components and nature of elements.

Then came the stunning theories and discoveries in physics that gave complete and detailed description to the origin of the universe and the motions of space objects. In addition to this, many other hypotheses about things that have not been discovered yet like the parallel universe.

On the other hand, these theories can explain what is made but cannot make what was explained by these theories; despite all the mathematical equations and all the technologies, humans were not able to create one quark or one living cell.

Or to give a clear idea of how this huge factory that contains everything was built, and by that factory I mean the universe.

Millions of people converted into atheism, and many had fought against it, many others criminalized and prohibited it. Debates between the two sides became very popular and each side gets excited when they find a proof or evidence that validates their point and their side.

Here I quote from someone who said .... 'God had created me in the best way possible and put me on the top of the pyramid of all creatures. He gave me a brain, awareness and I learned the most noble morals and good deeds. Now you want me to believe that nature created me by a coincidence? And the probability of that coincidence was 1 in ten billion? And I am equal to all other creatures in the wild? I would never accept that for myself.'

By the way, are humans the only intelligence species in the universe? And why???

A vast expanding universe that is estimated to measure around 90 billion light years across. So even if someone traveled at the speed of light they will never reach the edge of the universe because of the expansion. The universe itself is expanding at the speed of light. If you were to travel out of this universe, you will find other Parallel universes stretching at the speed of light. These many universes are awash with dark matter and dark energy.

If we take a look at earth we will find that it consists of rocks and sand, These in turn consists of some of the elements on the periodic table. Scientists were very happy when they discovered the molecular composition of these materials, they considered it to be a huge leap that will help explain more hypothesis in physics and chemistry as well as other elements reactions in nature.

But their celebration did not last long as they discovered that these molecules are made of smaller parts called atoms, then they discovered even smaller parts, the neutrons and protons. Then they found out that these in turn are made up of quarks, and there is another hypothesis that says that quarks cane be composed of smaller parts too. This means that if we looked at the sky we can observe a huge and almost an infinite universe, if we looked down below our feet we can observe that we look like giants standing on very small world.

(Is there creatures else out there except us in this huge universe?)

Humans keep asking this question but never looked at it from a different angle... a creature that has free will power and freedom, in addition to other scary traits like greed, ambition, love of control, and high readiness to commit anything no matter how horrible it is. Can't you see that this huge universe is the perfect place to imprison a creature with such qualities?!

"If science cannot prove a something; that does not mean it doesn't existing."

As a matter of fact, science does not deny religion or metaphysical phenomena, on the contrary, some of the texts from holy books that described certain metaphysical phenomena were later confirmed by scientific theories and mathematical facts.

Even atheism was not safe from being divided, as it has been divided into various and different philosophical groups, once it reached human hands.

The bottom line, The mistake is not in these things, I mean "religion or atheism" The mistake from misuse.

Now we will talk about another foundation of the human society.

((8))

Media

Media, or multimedia some people like to call it, was one of the factors that had the most effect on humans, whether positive or negative. Media focuses on the strongest human feelings and lyricism; Such as the love of appearance, fame, attention, influence, needs, money, and spreading ideas that make the mass trust and follow this or that media.

The first type of media was literature in all its types, especially poetry. That's why you usually see the most distinguished people leaning towards poets and philosophers, and rely on their ideas to gain people's trust and support, depending on the situation. It usually works.

Then the media machine evolved with advanced technology, so the modern media theories appeared. After that, some colleges adapted media classes as part of their courses.

Media methods increased and it became written, visual and as audio as well., It became very available for everyone. It is so accessible, you can use your smart phone to find anything you are looking for, whether that is news, reports, ads…etc.

The importance of media is in its effect on general public opinion and the way it directs these opinions (usually in the way that the owner or manager of this media wants).

As soon as a crisis starts to develop on the horizon, the preparation begins in secret. Then this terrific machine moves to do its role that has been calculated, and it can be used as a fatal weapon that is no less than deadly than actual weaponry and maybe even more powerful.

Because people trust numbers and statistics, the media tends to use them in times of crisis, it advertises all kinds of events the same way fire spread in a dry brush. The effects are hypnotic to people, and that usually guarantee the desired outcome. The general public would move in the di-rection that media wanted and planned for ahead of time.

Then many years after the fact, the media would intentionally report a calm version of the event. This report would simply state the previously mentioned report that was originated during the war or crisis, and indicates that it was not true and there is no evidence to support it.

What is that called??? I leave you to ponder what the right name or title for that is. The bitter sweet about this is there is no authority that can question or prosecute the people or media who fabricated these false news. Moreover, the same game is repeated in the next crisis.

This is the negative side of media that results from abusing something to reach certain aims and gains .....

But there is another good and noble side to some of the media, that all humanity is grateful for, We will talk about that tomorrow.

Another work day passed and at the end of the day we were waiting for our usual evening discussions. I noticed that people around me were quiet and did not talk much, when I ask "Hey, why are you quiet? Is there anything on your mind or bothering you?"

"Huh?, no no, everything is alright" I told my father about this and he said "This is normal son. We spoke about many important and crucial matters. We discussed future concerns about their lives and their children. Humans, by nature, are a worrying and anxious creature; unstable, at times. Once a human obtains what they want and reaches their immediate goal in their daily lives, then you see them calm, relaxed and happy for those moments of daily live. But when they undergo change due to a shift in circumstance or as a result of higher motivation, then you see them worried and quiet unlike the usual. A change towards the unknown is what worries humans the most, especially if that change implies more responsibilities for oneself and others around them. Don't worry son, I already thought of this and took it into consideration, and today I will talk about this topic."

We gathered in the evening at our usual spot. My father was smiling while looking at people's faces, then he started talking: "Dear families and friends, I was informed that you are perplexed by the advice and information that you heard from me yesterday, and are confused by my instructions regarding organizing our future society. Would you like me to stop? Maybe this will be better so you can take your time and relax? What do you think?"

The audience started muttering and they looked confused. "Stop? Why?" Did anyone complain? Why not stop and let everything be? Who knows the future and what variations it might carry? Alright, but we need to know. We need the previous knowledge and experience, so maybe this is the best chance to learn. "

When the audiences' side conversations became loud, my father spoke with a higher tone and said "Alright, alright, quiet please. Let me tell you something, then the decision is yours, ok?

As you know, the most difficult stages are the ones in the beginning, the stages of building the basis and foundation. Thus you notice that humans tend to need a huge motivation to make the decision to start.

What's more difficult is the planning and preparation stage that is the stage we are working on now. I initiated this matter, I am prepared for the level of responsibility that comes with it. Giving advice is something that may result in unpredictable consequences, I might get negative reactions. When you start advising someone, they initially listen to you, but then another part of that person's brain starts spinning and calculating both positive and negative questions. Usually the lions share belongs to the negative thoughts, in many cases, they overcome on the good and positive questions.

The positive thoughts: 'This is good.', 'I will try it anyway.', 'This makes sense.', 'It can make the situation better.', 'How much time till this becomes true?, etc. The negative (or dark?) thoughts: 'Does he think he is better than me to give me advice?', 'What will he gain from that?', 'How much would I lose in the beginning?', 'What I will doing if the situation become worse?'. These are few examples for both of these positive and negative thoughts.

It seems obviously clear to you that I am near the end of my life. The amount of food and drink I consume will not increase whether I am the most important or the least important person among you.

The main reason I am motivated to provide you guidance and put myself in this position of criticism and questioning, is because I have witnessed what happened at that time. I witnessed how civilization completely collapsed, utterly destroy, and billions of people died. I witnessed the destruction of great scientific achievements that took huge effort and a long time to create; it took thousands of scientists and thinkers to formulate. It was the end result of years of research and ideas. It cost large amounts of money and resources. Huge advances in many scientific and medical fields, evaporated in moments. For what??? Just so few people gain more benefits, higher positions, more money, or authority? Haha They bought so little but paid a huge price. I will not let this tragedy happen again. I used to scream at them, in vain: The luxuries, bliss, and technologies we are enjoying now are almost magical, keep them safe and do not take them for granted. We did not reach to this level easily, it was the result of our fathers and ancestors. This is an achievement that we have to preserve, please keep it, I beg you"

On the other hand, I do not blame you for worrying. We were created that way, we hold noble human morals deep inside. In addition to that, humans seek perfection in every detail of life, and when they face a change that force them to alter their morals and values...... it causes pain that starts

with a lower chest that radiates to the stomach and then keeps going down. Then after that, you feel weakness in the legs. Then you would gather your-self and begin what you wanted to do, and get rid of that moment of weak-ness. Then after a while, the over analyzing begins, and it can make you lose your appetite, lose sleep, lose interest in things like love, and every-thing would taste the same to you; bitter, fuscous, desperate and dark.,

Consciousness is responsible for this kind of thinking. It is the guard that never sleeps. It analyzes, search-es, organizes and evaluates things. Then it gives you the strict verdict towards yourself. If you have a live conscience you will live happily comfortable and have peace of mind. You will be content with your life, satisfied and have low income. Hahaha, well not necessarily.

However, if that guard was missing or asleep, which you don't want, then you can get infected with the most horrible traits, and commit the worst crimes. The more your conscience die, the more famous you become. Hahaha, I mean famous war criminals and serial killers, whose biography are filled with the stores of very bloody acts, whom have killed thousands of people, and in some cases millions of people, did not even blink an eye.

I elaborated a lot about con-scious-ness, and I did that because I noticed that you were concerned and had worries, which implies that you have good conscience, and high sense of responsibility towards yourselves and your families. This is an evident in happy successful families, when you see parents concerned about their children and about any little thing that might impact them. Dear compatri-ots, after this elaboration, I leave the choice for you. I am but a man who has some knowledge that I would like to pass to you, and if you want to accept it, that would make me really happy. If you want me to stop, then I will wish you a happy life and prosperous future. Take your time and I will wait your decision.

One day passed and no one showed up at the meeting spot. Then the next day everyone attended and they were in a very high spirit, very optimistic and joyful. One of them said: "Dear Sir, our brother and revered teacher, we appreciate your valuable lectures, and we would like to continue to listen to you to learn more. Your advice is priceless and we live in a time that such knowledge, advice, and wisdom are rare. My father smiled in content. "Thank you for your trust, I also appreciate you listening to me. I am simply giving you free advice; not orders. Thus you do not have to implement these suggestions. The choice is yours. I hope you use moderation when making decisions while staying flexible. Do not let your decision become a shackle around your neck that you cannot get out of. Haha. The only way to get out of it, in that case, is to break your own neck.

Alright, let's go back to our topic. We left off on the positive side of media, which is indeed an unparallel noble role. Media can be the voice of people, speaking on people's behalf and expressing their concerns and issues. It analyzes and demonstrates. Journalists offer a valuable favor to the human society. Some of them spend days and nights to write entire books by hand before the invention of typing. Some of them spent their entire life writing human literature and philosophy. Some of them took their cameras and traveled to hot or frozen spots around the world to cover events from there or write down scientific facts about creatures that live in such environments.

Some of them dove into the depths of the ocean, or climbed high mountains just to give us a glimpse of these magical views while we are sitting comfortably at home drinking tea, safe and sound, unaware of the huge efforts and will power for these people who spent months just to compile a video that lasts one hour. Some of them risk their lives to support a certain cause. Some were tortured and imprisoned or were sent to exile and were accused of high treason. Some of them paid the ultimate price and were shot or Slaughter with a knife just because they said the truth, supported a certain cause, or criticized a certain political view or dictator. These are the ones that I would consider the same level as martyrs and prophets. Prophets were tortured and killed because the spoke the truth and support the oppressed and called for justice, they are all the same, in my opinion.

((9))

Economics & Politics

Two siblings that cannot be separated. The relationship between them is like that of the brain and muscles.

They are the hidden hands that control and move the human society. All vocabulary of life are mere rivers that pour into the sea of politics. The art of articulate lying, the twisting of phrases, the dark alleys, the switching of sides, and the ability to change colors thousands of times better than the chameleon. Contradicting themselves as long as their interests requires that.

One time you see them defending a certain idea fiercely, and gather people behind their opinions using media and all other possible ways, but when things change, anyone who dares to speak about that same idea will suffer their wrath!!!!! No wonder that is what the current events requires. They invented the ownership and the inheritance of ruling and governing, so that the ruling family does not lose any benefits. The most horrifying and un-imaginable crimes were committed in the name of the throne. Some kings and rulers killed those who were closest to them, even family members, in cold blood, just because they stood in their way, conspired against them, or tried to take their throne.

So what would happen to the general public???? The ruler might have mercy on them but that's not more than the mercy of a shepherd on his sheep and cash cows!!! They revolted against the kingship, the tyrannical system of passing the authority from parents to offspring.

But if a certain sects settled in their reign, what would be the best way to control the authority in a democratic shape that does not provoke the general public opinion and the word on the streets?????Ruling political parties are the solution.

Have you seen any democratic country, with regular election periods, whose politics changed with every new elected president? Of course not.

I had wished if one of my students have a high presidential position, so I can give that student a quiz and tell him: "Mr. president, or your highness the king or the sultan, can you answer the following: a head of a household of 3, has the responsibility and bur-den of 3 people, that responsibility is increased by the increase of the family members. So how do you feel when you have the responsibility and burden of millions???" How does your consciousness feel when you sleep warm with full belly, while one of your people have starved or are frozen when sleeping? Have you asked yourself why the authority that was given to you had placed you above the law? Or made you better than your people which you could not been in this position without them.

Is it fair that your people live comfortably and enjoy luxuries on the expense of the lives and blood of other nations?"

The topic of politics is similar to religion, as both depend on the morals of the person himself.

As far as economics, it is the executing hands of politics. I will continue talking about this topic tomorrow.

Good night.

((10))

My father started with his speech: "We spoke a lot about the basis of the human society and the proper ways to adapt and apply these basis to humans themselves. Now let's take a look at the topic from a different perspective and ask the following question: 'Why do we see miserable and broken people despite them living in a good society??? We are not saying ideal society, just a good society.

Some people get the chance to succeed and be happy, but they did not take the opportunity to do so. The answer is simple and clear.

Success depends on the individual and not the society.

Here I would like to address few things that I believe to be important to pay attention to for each individual.

((11))

Time

This stealth creature that moves silently and has no color or taste or smell. It is delicious, light, and fast when you spend it in a fun way or with someone you love. But it is heavy and slow and bitter if you have work to be done or are waiting for something to happen.

Humans cannot control it, and they can only divide it so they know how to get paid or pay their debts, and to record different occasions. They use names for months and days and years, use a calendar with the same diving system yet follow different start dates. Whether that is the birth or a special person, or an important event for certain nation, or the foundation or a political party, or the crowning of a tyrant who is very controlling of his people, as the Parable says "the reasons vary but the calendar is one". Some people know its value, thus they divide it into nanoseconds. Others don't know how much time they have wasted.

It has a very annoying trait, it goes only in one direction and cannot change that no matter how hard you try. And by that, it differs from its other siblings, the 3 dimensions.

You have limited time, that is undisputed fact, but no one knows when that time limit ends. As I said, once you feel it flying fast, and other times going so slow, depending on the circumstances.

The important point here is to be ready physically and mentally to take advantage of the right moment, that is your responsibility. You must also secure the other peoples' needs. In other words, you must seize the moment in a productive way when you have the requirements to do so, when you have someone who helps you complete your other daily needs.

Parents sacrifice their comfort and efforts and time, so the parents pro-vi-

de time for their children to pro-vi-
de benefit to them. Is it fair that this
precious time is wasted in vain? Pay
attention.

((12))

Money

These magical colorful papers that comes after huge efforts and sweat, and after spending a lot of time exhausting oneself at many jobs. Effort, commitment, and order, it may or may not be a good working atmosphere. You may or may not like the people you work with, some of them might work against you in public and behind closed doors.

Many of them want legitimate profit, but whomever goes down the wrong path will only have themselves to blame. Some people are simply talented. Once you give them a chance to work, they turned that opportunity into a profitable trade. Some others just inherited that fortune. Both would have plenty of these colorful papers at hand, some of them would fall in the trap of spending and become a sibling to devils for being an over-spender.

I do not disagree with these people, as they have the right to enjoy the profit they made. They worked hard for it.

Two questions to ask yourself while you are spending money.

The first is, have I given the fair share to whomever deserves some of this money? My family and children??

The second question is..... Will this money be as available and plentiful tomorrow as it today?????

((13))

Love then marriage
OR
Marriage then love

Here I used the word THEN not AND. (And) refers to connecting two similar or different things, while (then) refers to sequence between two relevant things. That shows the connection between love and marriage. The main motive is love; whether it is true love or just infatuation.

Love is that state that makes the person do the impossible so easily that it surprises that person themselves, and makes them wonder "Did I really do that?" No, no, hahaha... That is not possible. How did I do that??? No, I think I can succeed if I try again???" These questions usually come after the accomplishment itself and after reaching the goal.

Love is like politics when I said "All vocabulary of the human society drains into the river of politics.", so does love, as it is the motivation for doing almost everything. Psychologists have mentioned that "Ninety percent of the human motivations are sexual."

I want to work and save money so I can be with the woman of my dreams.

I must finish my studies, and then graduate, and then get married. I will become attractive to many women when I grow my muscles. Again 90% of the motivation of work and achievements have a sexual incentive, while the remaining 10% is the share of great people and their great immortal achievements.

Life is wonderful, the pleasures and blessings are almost infinite. The most wonderful part is to share these blessings and pleasures with someone, then bring beautiful children to this wonderful life. This childish spontaneous moments that is unparallel in its beauty, makes people get on their knees to play with children, and go back in time to act like children too. Sometimes they even forget their social standing as they break character and roll on the ground to play with a dominating effect of childhood, and without any shame or embarrassment.

On contrary, they are filled with joy and happiness for these wonderful moments that they spent playing with this or that child. This is the fruit of love, the noble aim and honorable path, the sublime purpose of humans on this planet.

When you get married, you invest everything you earned in your life, all the money, knowledge, and inheritance from your parents or grandparents. Of course you want your existence and what you gained to be useful for your family and children after you. So they become a branch of that tree, and that creek of that great river.

This is love, words and pages are not enough to describe it.

Then... marriage. Hahaha. That poor creature that you once see cursed as Satan and is being described with the worst traits. "The biggest mistake, killer mistake, ooh if I can turn back time, unavoidable evil, to get married or to not get married... either way you will regret....etcetera."

The second situation is when you see it being described as divine nectar that came directly from heaven. It is described with the most wonderful words. The medicine for every disease.

So which one is the true definition?? Are they talking about the same thing?? What a puzzle!! Are humans all insane to describe one thing with such contradictory words?

The truth is, both contradictory words can apply on marriage depending on the situation. That is not a de-scription but rather a living situation where a person describes what happened under the circumstances of a marriage. Thus, if that person was successful in their choice, then they would feel afloat on heavenly honey. But if that person was not successful in their choice, then they will sink in that honey but only after dying from the sting of the bees in the beehive the person placed themselves in.

So be very careful when you choose your life partners, this is not a commodity that you can replace or return, it is a priceless part of your life, it is your existence that you are exchanging with your partner. It is a heavy debt and huge responsibility to take on, in order to start a happy family.

Happy marriage relies on two main basis and cannot succeed without them; attention and respect between the spouses.

Tomorrow we will talk about the family.

Goodnight

((14))

The Family

That beautiful structure. The establishment that offers everything you could dream about; possessions, food, comfy residence, love, passion, and effective help in many different situations. When you get sick you will have someone to help you, when you are sad you have someone to comfort you, when you are outside your house feeling down, you know that once you get back home to your family that sadness will melt away. All these emotion-al and financial services for free!! Wow that sounds wonderful.

What do you have to give in return for all of this? Practically nothing.

All you have to do is to form your own family to provide the same ser-vices for your family members. That way you would have repaid the services that you received from your family, and the life cycle continues.

Some people live happily among their families, especially when the parents are ideal and provide for their children with all the elements required to succeed and feel comfortable. Others suffer among their families if the parents were suffering from difficult life circumstances or one of them is not up to the responsibility or have a mistaken concept about how to manage a family.

Those two types are much better than the others without families. This used to happen a lot in most societies because of the liberated relation-ships between the two genders for the purpose of sexual pleasure and fun. These relationships that are not governed by any agreed upon bond be-tween the two people, and by that I mean marriage, and the furthermore is that "They consider children who are born out of these relationships to be a side effect, that may or may not happen. Side effect??????

You do understand that you are talking about a human being, a fresh, green, innocent a creature. What is the fate of that baby? How much attention and care would that baby get? Can fresh green sprouts (babies) grow in the desert? Let's suppose it can grow in the desert, what will it produce?"

I cannot forget the letters that I received from a friend, a specialist in social sciences, who was called into a re-habilitation center in faraway country. He wrote to me a lot about the cases that he treated. One of his letters read:

((How are you doing my dear friend? I still miss you dearly. I miss our good conversations and your way of giving advice. When I was called for this job, I was very happy as I have the opportunity to help people overcome the issues and crises they went through and suffered from. It is a wonderful feeling when you feel as a useful human that participate in this wonderful life, and help others overcome their trouble and start fresh.

I left good memories in the hearts of many people I treated, but they left a sad and painful memory in mine. They did not do that on purpose at all. It is my fault that I let their issues affect me. It could be my naivety. Maybe I was too nice. I remember you mocked me for these traits. Or it could be the miserable life that these people went through that make even the toughest hearts soften and the eyes shed tears of blood. How would you feel when you sit down with someone while they share how they met their life partner and started an intimate relationship that carried many beautiful dreams about happiness, settling and great achievements, such as starting a family and children who are happy and feel secure because their parents are there to take care of them and raise them to become useful citizens in society. In turn they will make their parents proud of them.

All these Sweet pink dreams, which is the right for everyone to dream, will vanish and turn into a dark nightmare a miserable life full of suffering and loneliness, facing a brutal world that has no mercy, bills and requirements piling...etc.

Add for that caring for one or more children from a previous relationship, when the exranaway during a starless night. How harsh is your heart to do such a thing???? Have you thought of the future of people whom you left behind to face the storm of life alone? Can you imagine the psychological state of a child who lives without one of the parents?? That child might will grow up missing the role model of a teacher or mentor, that child may become an easy prey for loss, poverty, and deprivation. A young soul that carries more burden that it can handle, and has to survive on its own. Such children might have to drop out of school and work as vendors in the streets to sup-port themselves and whomever is de-pendent on them. They get as dirty as the street they work in.

Note: Street children is a phenomenon that is widely spreads in poor countries. While the developed countries have good social security system to prevent that. Children are lucky in this case.

This is an important case that we must pay attention to. Children might miss the chance to experience their childhood because of the living circumstances. When these children grow up and get married and have their own children, they won't be able to understand the real meaning of childhood or its requirements.

The saddest part is, this child might grow up to repeat the same sad story (or tragedy) with their partner!!! This is what bewilders me!!!

Logic suggests that no one gives what they do not have (nemo dat principle), damn... this is true and makes sense, but it is not enough to silence the voice of consciousness and its constant nagging deep into the soul.

It is not enough for the conscious mind that makes judgments and analyzes the smallest of matters.

Nemo dat principle..... but you are

not obligated to oppress someone else and repeat the same crime that was committed against you, thus you become both the oppressed an the oppressor.

Silence…. Is the answer to my question every time I sit down and worked with one of them.

You could have formed a successful family that fulfils all the dreams, but why didn't you?????

That is the last of my friend letters and his speech about the family. Goodnight.

((15))

We continued doing this for a long time, we met with my father and discussed things. We clarified a few previous topics, or made decisions and so on, depending on the situation. After a while, my father's health deteriorated and his activities decreased. His last words stayed in our minds. "I have lived a long eventful life. I am satisfied with it. Now I look at my clock on this earth and see that I am running out of time minutes and seconds are getting slower and eventually will stop. The certain fate for every creature is to perish. Hahaha. Some people seek and dream of immortality. Just to satisfy infinite pleasure and lusts, of which humans can't get enough from it. Some of them lose track of the real goal and purpose of existence, thus wasting precious time of their lives. Each of us have an important role in this life.

The closest example I can think of is if you imagine the human to be a golden block that is used to pave a long road where a beautiful great queen walks Dignity and majesty. This is the life.

I advise you of this, being content is like owning an infinite treasure. It can make you happy and content with whatever you have, even if it wasn't much. It can make you patient at the most difficult and stressing situations.

God created the stomach to be content with any food that enters it, it does not complain if the food was cheap and does not dance in joy if the food was expensive. Simplicity, contentment, and satisfaction are the keys to happiness and peace of mind, if you have these you will live in heaven on earth.

There is nothing more wonderful than going to sleep with a relieved mind, peace of mind, no one had suffered or cried because of you that you might have nightmares of and start seeing flashbacks during every aspect of your life.

I have mentioned in the beginning that I have lived a long eventful life, the period I spent with you was the best and I wish to love longer to enjoy it more, but it is a sealed fate. I wish you and your predecessors a happy and joyful life."

The people started to tear up, and they said "We thank you for all the advice and instructions you gave us, and rest assured that your words will be a guide, just like a lighthouse guides ships at night during heavy storm to help these ships reach the safe harbor and save them from the deadly rocks. We feel honored to have talked with you and enjoyed in your speeches."

Few days later, my father passed away peacefully and quietly. He was gone but his words remained. The life went on.... As usual.

((16))

Author's final word

Dear reader... thank you for reaching these lines. After your journey in my book, I don't know what type of impressions my book had left on your mind?! But I want to say that I wrote a completely novel without any names, there had been no names of people, places, religions, political party, or any other proper nouns. Things are named by their public, not private, names. thus no one can accuse me I wrote to support this team or that team.

No one paid me to write this book, my motivation was the suffering we went through in the past. We still witness painful and violent scenes for people being tortured, dismembered, and burnt alive. We see them on the screens and can hear their screams, cries and weeps clearly. That leaves a permanent memory in the mind, as permanent as being branded by fire. Your pain increases as you try to dis-cover the reasons for such crimes, only to find out it was a lame excuse to burn someone alive.

Sometimes you see people suffering from being overweight who try to be on diets who live on the expense of people who never had any digestive issues or a heartburn.

Bottom line is, there is no accept-able reason or excuse to bring suffering and misery to others.

All traits exist within you…. But only you know which traits are more dominant than others.

Since you have all these traits, then you can transform and change, I am not saying changing is easy, but it is possible.

When I listed the basis of the human society, I was referring to people not specialties.

When you have a position you have the authority because of that position. So please make your effect positive on others. Do not go after person-al gain that makes others suffer because of you.

Now, at the final lines of this book, I asked myself few questions

Was I the first person to write a book that urges people to do good??? The answer is ...NO

Am I the last person who will write a book that urges people to do good??? The answer is ...NO

So what's new in your book that gave us headaches and you spent Thirty-six months in writing??? The answer is... NOTHING.

Of course there's nothing new, as most writers have urged people to do good, they did so in writing and in other ways. No one had come up with a new thing, because good deeds in all their details, as well as bad deeds, are very clear to everyone.

You, dear reader, are like a shopper at a big bazaar, that found all types of merchandise, so be careful what you pick, as there will be someone outside to judge you when you leave the market.

But me, and the others across the ages, who urged people to do good, they are just reminders and nothing more.

The end